Òran

Owen Sutcliffe

methuen | drama

LONDON · NEW YORK · OXFORD · NEW DELHI · SYDNEY

METHUEN DRAMA

Bloomsbury Publishing Plc, 50 Bedford Square, London, WC1B 3DP, UK
Bloomsbury Publishing Inc, 1359 Broadway, New York, NY 10018, USA
Bloomsbury Publishing Ireland, 29 Earlsfort Terrace, Dublin 2, Ireland

BLOOMSBURY, METHUEN DRAMA and the
Methuen Drama logo are trademarks of Bloomsbury Publishing Plc

First published in Great Britain 2025

A catalogue record for this book is available from the British Library.

Library of Congress Control Number: 2025945606

ISBN: PB: 978-1-3506-0492-6
         ePDF: 978-1-3506-0493-3
         eBook: 978-1-3506-0494-0

Series: Modern Plays

Typeset by Westchester Publishing Services
Printed and bound in Great Britain

For product safety related questions contact productsafety@bloomsbury.com.

To find out more about our authors and books visit
www.bloomsbury.com and sign up for our newsletters.

Òran

Owen Sutcliffe

Òran – 2025 Tour Creative Team

Writer	**Owen Sutcliffe**
Director	**Jack Nurse**
Performer	**Robbie Gordon**
Music	**VanIves & Ben Deans**
Lighting Designer	**Benny Goodman**
Video Designer	**Heather Scott**
Technician	**Cécile Segura**
Production Manager	**Suzie Normand**
Marketing	**Serden Salih**
Press & Publicity	**Michelle Mangan**
Assistant Producer	**Yexabel Rivero**

Owen Sutcliffe Writer

Owen is a writer, emcee and youth worker based in Glasgow. He is a writer in residence with the Edinburgh Book Festival and was the National Theatre of Scotland's 2025 'Discover' resident. Owen is a national prizewinner in Gaelic poetry and his work has been published in *Northwords Now* and *Gutter*. He is also a hip-hop emcee, releasing music under the moniker CRPNTR and as one half of the duo tues.

Jack Nurse Director

Jack is a director and theatre-maker. He co-founded Glasgow-based theatre company Wonder Fools in 2014.

In 2024, Wonder Fools won Best Debut at The Skinny's Besties Awards (for *Òran*), were finalists in The Stage Awards for Community Project of the Year (for Positive Stories for Negative Times) and became one of Creative Scotland's Regularly Funded (Multi-Year) Organisations.

Training: Royal Conservatoire of Scotland and the National Theatre Studio Directors' Course

As writer: *Same Team: A Street Soccer Story* (Traverse Theatre)

As director/writer: *549: Scots of the Spanish Civil War*, *The Kelton Hill Fair*, *The Coolidge Effect* (Wonder Fools); *When the Sun Meets the Sky* (Traverse Theatre/Capital Theatres)

As director: *24 (Day): The Measure of My Dreams*, *The Essence of the Job Is Speed* (Almeida Theatre); *Òran*, *And Then Come the Nightjars* (Wonder Fools); *Lampedusa* (Citizens Theatre/Wonder Fools); *Meet Jan Black* (Wonder Fools/The Gaiety); *Larchview* (National Theatre of Scotland/BBC Scotland); *The Lost Elves* (Citizens Theatre/RCS); *The Mack*, *The Storm* (A Play, A Pie and A Pint/Traverse Theatre)

www.jacknurse.com

Robbie Gordon Performer

Robbie is a Scottish theatre-maker, writer and creative engagement specialist based in Glasgow. Born in Prestonpans, he trained at the Royal Conservatoire of Scotland, graduating in 2016 with the Drama in Education Award. He is the co-founder and Co-Artistic

Director of Wonder Fools, a socially engaged theatre company creating bold new work with communities across Scotland and beyond. Robbie's practice focuses on making theatre that is accessible, political and rooted in real-life stories – from international participatory projects to critically acclaimed stage plays.

Recent work includes *Same Team, Òran, 549: Scots of the Spanish Civil War, Tether* and *The Kelton Hill Fair*. He also leads Positive Stories for Negative Times, an international participatory programme that has reached over 12,000 young people in twenty-four countries and has commissioned twenty-two new plays by some of the UK's most exciting artists. He was formerly Creative Engagement Director at the Traverse Theatre in Edinburgh and The Gaiety in Ayr.

In 2024, Wonder Fools won Best Debut at The Skinny's Besties Awards, were finalists in The Stage Awards for Community Project of the Year and became one of Creative Scotland's Regularly Funded (Multi-Year) Organisations. 2025 sees a programme of four new groundbreaking productions and four PSFNT festivals across Scotland.

Ben Deans Composer

Ben is a musician, producer and community worker based in Glasgow. He has performed across the UK and Europe in a range of musical projects. As a director of anam creative, he is working to create meaningful opportunities for artists across Scotland.

VanIves Composers

VanIves' music is for sunsets and sunrises, for long car journeys and coffee shop corners. They translate their love for their quaint Scottish home and life-affirming experiences into cathartic songwriting and nostalgic tones.

The alt/pop, Glasgow-based span multi-genres, taking the audience on a journey to memorable moments, from brotherly harmonies and euphoric pop choruses to experimental genre-exploring builds.

VanIves' debut album *Thanks* was premiered on BBC Radio 1 by Gemma Bradley in 2022 and picked up by editorial playlists like Spotify's 'The Most Beautiful Songs in the World' and 'New Music Friday'. The album launch at Òran Mór in Glasgow was sold out. VanIves reached the final of the BBC Introducing Scottish Act of the

Year and performed on the BBC Introducing stage at the Latitude Festival. The band kicked off 2023 with a sold-out headline festival slot at Celtic Connections at St Luke's.

VanIves have grown together over the years, playing hundreds of live shows and spending countless hours experimenting in their DIY studio to create something unique, honest and powerful.

Benny Goodman Lighting Designer

Benny is a freelance lighting designer based in Glasgow and London. He has worked in theatres across the UK and Europe in a variety of projects and productions, and is a creative collaborator with theatre company Wonder Fools.

Selected credits include: *The Mountaintop* (Lyceum Theatre); *Gods of Salford* (Not Too Tame/Lowry Theatre); *When Prophecy Fails* (Groupwork); *Treasure Island* (Scottish Theatre Producers); *Twelfth Night* (Shakespeare North); *Aganeeza Scrooge* (Tron Theatre); *Beauty and the Beast, Cinderella, Snow White* (Bard in the Botanics/Byre Theatre); Four Walls (Derby Theatre); *La Performance* (Tron Theatre/Paris IVT); *A Midsummer Night's Dream* (Orange Tree Theatre); *Hamlet* (Saint Stephen's Theatre); *Hang* (Tron Theatre); *Sense of Centre* (Dance Base, Edinburgh); *Julius Caesar* (Company of Wolves Scottish tour); *Palace of Varieties* (Derby Theatre); *Learning from the Future* (OGR Torino); *The Tempest* (Tron Theatre); *Meet Jan Black* (The Gaiety); *Maim* (Tron Theatre); *I Can Go Anywhere* (Traverse Theatre); *The Drift* (National Theatre of Scotland); *The Afflicted* (Summerhall); *Country Music* (Omnibus Theatre); *549: Scots of the Spanish Civil War* (UK tour); *The Mistress Contract* (Tron Theatre); *Daddy Drag* (Assembly Roxy); *Where We Are: The Mosque* (Arcola Theatre); *Sorella Mia* (The Place); *Disarming Reverberations* (St Giles' Cathedral, Edinburgh); *Heroines* (Theatre Gu Leor, Stornoway); *Humbug* (Tramway); *Snow Queen* (Associate – Dundee Rep); *Like Animals* (Tron Theatre); *Ayanfe, a Yoruba Opera* (Bridewell Theatre); *Lampedusa* (Citizens Theatre); *Circle of Fifths* (Tron Theatre/Cockpit Theatre)

Heather Scott Video Designer

Heather (she/her) is excited for *Òran* to be her first professional credit as video designer, having started as a Video Design Intern at the National Theatre of Scotland on the production of *Burn* (2022). For the past three years she has worked on both national and international productions. Recent associate credits include: *The Great Gatsby* (London Coliseum and GS Arts Center, Seoul); *Just for One Day* (Mirvish Theatre, Toronto and Shaftesbury Theatre, London); *Starlight Express* (Troubadour Wembley Park Theatre). Being a Glasgow local, Heather is extremely proud to be working on a Scottish production as her professional debut.

Cécile Segura Technician

Cécile (she/her) holds the wizardry behind Hades' voice and the lift's operation. She lives and works in Glasgow as a live sound engineer and production manager. She is committed to socially engaged performances advocating and facilitating accessible, feminist, LGBTQ+ and decolonial cultural events.

Cécile has studied Interaction Design at the Glasgow School of Art and classical violin at the Conservatoire in Lyon. She regularly collaborates with Wonder Fools (production manager and operator: *Òran*; stage manager and operator: *Alright Sunshine*; operator: *549: Scots of the Spanish Civil War*).

Cécile's work has been broadcast on TV by the BBC and France Television and reached the top 15 of the German charts in 2022. She was awarded the Scottish Alternative Music Award in 2020, the Best Debut at The Skinny's Besties Awards with Wonder Fools in 2024, the Edinburgh Innovation Award in 2024, and has been funded by the Lesbians of Public Interest.

Suzie Normand Production Manager

Suzie is one half of SNC Productions, which was established in 2023 with Craig Fleming. Their mission is to offer the highest-quality production and tour management support to Scotland's small and mid-scale touring sector. Suzie and Craig bring together over fifty years' combined experience working across Scotland's theatre sector, most notably with Catherine Wheels Theatre Company where they created and toured multi-award-winning theatre productions across Scotland, the UK and internationally. Recent clients include National Theatre of Scotland, Scottish Opera, Royal Lyceum Theatre, Freckle Productions, Lung Ha, Dundee Rep, Scottish Dance Theatre,

Scottish Theatre Producers, Foresight Theatrical, Noise Maker, Macrobert Arts Centre, Platform, Wonder Fools, Curious Seed, 21 Common, Starcatchers, Guesthouse and Stellar Quines.

Serden Salih Marketing

Serden is a freelance marketing and communications manager with over ten years' experience in theatre, film and events. He previously worked as Distribution Manager at Peccadillo Pictures, one of the UK's leading LGBT film distributors. Projects he has worked on have been shown at major festivals including Berlin International Film Festival, FrightFest London, BFI London Film Festival, BFI Flare, Edinburgh Festival Fringe and Edinburgh International Film Festival. In theatre, Serden has collaborated with Wonder Fools, Traverse Theatre, Sleeping Warrior, Superfan Performance, Barrowland Ballet and ThickSkin Theatre, delivering impactful and successful marketing campaigns.

Yexabel Rivero Assistant Producer

Yexabel enjoys many aspects of the creative industry, and bringing ideas to life. Whether it's curating events that connect Scotland's vibrant creative community, crafting stories through editing or working on the production side of filmmaking, she sees every project as an opportunity to explore and create.

Yexabel's belief in the arts' power to connect people and share diverse perspectives has shaped her career. Her background in media production spans short and long-form scripted films, documentaries, live events and advertising. Expanding her work beyond the screen industries, she now also works in theatre and community events. She also co-runs Unknown Errors, a platform which champions creatives in the community and offers a collective healing space for artists to process, share and generate positive change.

ABOUT WONDER FOOLS

Wonder Fools are a socially engaged theatre company and registered charity (SC047673).

Vision

High-quality arts experiences for everyone.

Mission

As a socially engaged theatre company we:

- Make work with communities that has national ambition and mass appeal.
- Equip artists to deliver socially engaged arts projects.

We do this to achieve the following:

- Broaden access to theatre for those who do not usually get the opportunity to engage.
- Empower young people through the arts.

What we do

Wonder Fools (WF) are a socially engaged theatre company and registered charity.

Since its inception in 2017, Wonder Fools has a proven track record of delivering high-quality arts projects through the three strands of our programme:

- co-creating ambitious theatre productions with young people and communities
- producing innovative artist development initiatives
- delivering ground-breaking creative engagement projects

Our productions have received critical acclaim and generated significant social impact. Highlights include:

- *549: Scots of the Spanish Civil War* – 'A formidable piece of popular small-scale touring theatre in the 7:84 tradition' (**** *The Scotsman*);
- The award-winning *Òran* – 'An electric one-man tour de force' (***** *The Arts Dispatch*);
- *The Events* – 'Demands to be seen' (**** *The Stage*).

Our flagship programme, Positive Stories for Negative Times (PSFNT), has been described as 'an astonishing youth theatre initiative' by *The Scotsman*. PSFNT has engaged over 13,000 young people across 24 countries since 2020. In a recent evaluation of PSFNT Season Three, 98% of participants reported increased confidence in drama-based activities, 100% of leaders observed skill development in their groups and 78% of leaders noted improved access to culture for young people.

Website: www.wonderfools.org Instagram: @wonder_fools_online
Facebook: /Wonder Fools Online Bluesky: @wonderfools.org
TikTok: @wonder_fools_online X: @wonder_fools

WONDER FOOLS TEAM

Robbie Gordon: Co-Founder & Artistic Director

Jack Nurse: Co-Founder & Artistic Director

Serden Salih: Head of Marketing & Communications

Sally Rennie: Finance & Admin Manager

WONDER FOOLS YOUTH BOARD

Aaron Clason

Aimee Parrett

Alexandra Finnie

Ami Hume

Annabel Lunney

Audrey Daines

Cara Slavin

Eilidh Smith

Ellen Bradbury

Emma Arbon

Gabrielle Monica

Genna Allan

Hannah McGregor

Indra Wilson

Isla MaClean

Katie Slater

Lauren Weir

Louis Gallagher

Manu Abeysuriya

Molly McGrath

Morgan Ferguson

Morgan Woods

Neve Adams

Roisin Barry

Tiger Mitchell

Uyi Uty

WONDER FOOLS BOARD OF TRUSTEES

The autumn 2025 tour of Òran is funded by Creative Scotland's Touring Fund.

Writer's Note

Òran is the first character I wrote for stage and I'm really fond of him. There's a lot in the play about the social circumstances of young people, the thorny road of growing, family trauma, the light and shade of social media and our lives online; but really, for me, it's a show about friendship. About good pals.

I've worked with young people in a variety of contexts and across a spectrum of ages and abilities for a decade, and I suppose this feeds my writing of characters like Òran. I'm probably in there somewhere, too, though I'm ashamed to say I'm not sure I'd be brave enough to take the lift. I love my pals, though. Fiercely.

I can't thank Jack Nurse and Robbie Gordon enough. In commissioning this play they gave me a rare opportunity, and their dramaturgical support helped establish *Òran*'s ultimate shape. Wonder Fools are an important company, a big-hearted bunch who walk the talk and then some.

Òran

Owen Sutcliffe

One

A phone rings, no answer. Then an answer machine plays:
'Please leave your message . . .'

Òran
The leaves are changing:
candlestick-brass, sandy and sunset,
auburn, shit-brown – autumn's in town.
They're in piles ripe for kicking,
scooped into wee tornadoes by the quick wind.

We used to skip into those tornadoes in primary school.
Mind?
We'd be right in the middle, crisp bags and juice straws
sucked up with the leaves
and all about us like wasps.
If any of it touched you, you were out.
Mind?
Euan?
You were a wizard in that wind.

We were pals then. And we were pals later
when we got bikes and they'd not expect us in until tea.
We built those dens in the mine woods and climbed
naked branches.
I broke my wrist falling and you pedalled back for Dad,
and the car
and they shook yellow leaves out my jacket at the hospital.

We were pals then. And we were pals later
when that first frost meant blue hands, 'cause if you're cool
you don't wear gloves.
Fumbling roll-ups, no-luck grown-ups wanting kissed
at the skate-park.
Autumn became quicker hiding places in the dinner-dark.

The leaves are changing
the pockets are plenty in my new jacket,
the moon's magic . . .
but I miss you.

It's new here without you.
Autumn's still nice and fresh
but I like it less without you.
The stars are out. I've saved you space
but you're ages late. I hope you're sleeping.
I wondered when to miss you most and chose the evening.

Shift.

Here . . . weren't we so proud when we got phones?
We'd be guarding our chargers like children.
They marked us part of something.
They flipped up then snapped sharp shut like bear traps –
Mum couldn't bear that.

You got so quick to reach, so easy to find.
We learned the spice of always-talk, curtains always drawn
but always not.
We grew new thumbs and were warmed by quick info,
in-jokes, ringtones.

You set Alan Partridge as your text alert!
Mind?
AHAAAA

But we learned too
the gut-rot of slow reply, the cruel insight of no invite.
I came to know how pale my penis was – how frail, how
un-American.
When bullies bullied they'd be doing it on phones
and we'd be in blanket-forts viewing it at home.
And our folks found out of course, yes,
and spun and wept and barely slept
but phones grew thin and blinked and crept
like fog fingers between our bones and legs

and tugged our growing hearts and heads . . .
they hardly rest . . .

Shift.

See me? I'm dog daft.
Faced with dog walker and dog stuck on separate log rafts
I'd save dog first and not-dog last.

Dad got us one when I was six
and six is young to bag shit and tag ticks, but I did.
And I loved the soft body, the hot breath: *Ob*sessed.

I think folk would say I'm sound enough.
Not Dad, but he's out of touch,
he'd say I'm honest like him and that Mum's proud of us,
even though she's always out and shouts and stuff.

Shift.

Thing about Mum is she'd been one already . . .
To Liam.

She'd already briefly been Mum
and in photos from then she looked fun.
We don't talk about Liam though,
unless it's just me and Dad.
Even then he gets sad.
Cos if Mum had already been Mum,
Dad had already been Dad.

I'd have been a wee brother you see.
And Mum doesn't try to be not nice to me,
but Dad says she's just injured inside, so she hides.

Shift.

Dad says Liam drew great wolves,
all fur and fluorescent drool.
And they'd take up a whole A4 cage
and seem alive on the page.

I learned about the wolves
after I drew one at school
and framed it and everything
and took it big out my bag
and Mum's eyes said, I don't like it,
and I don't much like you.
And Dad strung a sad string on it
and gave me a pat and said:
Let's hang it up after tea shall we?
But we never did.

And at Mum's Birthday Bingo
I cleaned all the windows,
invited the neighbours, made bunting from paper,
and Mum seemed okay till she tumbled away, and told
everyone . . . everyone:
It just doesn't feel the same with Òran.

It just doesn't feel the same with Òran.

Pause.

Dad would say I'm honest, he made me promise,
and I try to be . . .
It's just that when you weren't free to visit
I always stuck close to the boys
who seemed biggest.

But you, Euan . . . you were different:

Shift.

When the others stole Colm Shinty's shoes
and threw them across the river midwinter
you walked the long way round to get them.
When Martha Bea came back
after summer with new braces
and the others mocked and threw raisins
you sat next to her at lunch
and took a punch and the bruise faded.
      That was you: bravest.

When Hazel got the dates wrong
and came to school in fancy dress and sat and wept
you changed at break and told her with a painted face
we all make mistakes.
     That was you: caped.

But also, when they made us ask girls
across the hall to waltz
your shoulders lifted high to help you hide,
and I watched you, all at once, pull off a whole fingernail.
When groups gelled and swelled and fought
and swam without tops in summer lochs
and coupled off to cupboards locked
you said you felt your stomach knot,
and sat aside, cartoon-eyed.
     That was you: shy.

And so – you hid, so you did.

You started snapping at my hi's and why's
and blinking quicker, skipping dinner to cross
between worlds.
You'd show me what you typed in virtual rooms
where error soon meant lead balloon
and a lifetime in the stocks
and you'd been using words
like *fat* and *cock*.

There were boys onscreen
with plooks like yours
and you commented:
G O B L I N
M I N G E R
it was bruise or get bruised
so you grew crude fingers.

Shift, ominous.

Then one grey day you told me,
Someone online suggested you drink bleach to try and sleep
and film it for science week

and they'd get the whole street to donate a fiver each.
When you refused, confused
That someone wrote:

'Fine, no problem, here's the other option
We'll leak pictures of you wanking,
trying to practise with a condom.
You've sent them.
We've got them.'

Pause.

And when you told me this ugly thing
your face did a crumple thing
Your face did a hundred things
none of them comforting.

And so, burrowing down,
further down, into that new world,
you hid, seeming so much more sad than seething.
    And that was you: leaving.

Shift.

Now it's new here
without you.
Autumn's still nice and fresh but I like it less
without you.
The stars are out,
I've saved you space but you're ages late.
I hope you're sleeping.
I'm not sure I can handle
All these lonely evenings.

Òran *sags, morose, alone, contemplating the future. Then, after a
beat or two, lights and music shift and cue* **Hades.**

Hades
Òran. Òran.
You want him back don't you?
Your wee bestie.

Wee Euan.

You might just find him down here, if you look.
In the longest line.
We'd love to have you.

Pause, chuckles.

There's a bang of shitebag off you, Òran.
Always has been.

Òran
I'm no shitebag,
I'm not like that.

Hades
Well, then –
You know the way.
You've felt it.

It's there, always nearby, deep as shame.

The 'lift' lights up, **Òran** *inspects.*

Òran
A lift . . .

Hades
There's three stops on this journey, pal.
Three before you're downstairs –
Deep Downstairs –
and the real fun starts there.

Get honest though, Òran.
You'll not have him home otherwise.
When you find him, if you find him . . .
tell him.

Òran

Unconvincing.

Tell him what?

Hades

Tutting.

You know what.

Now go on – take the lift.
Press the button.

Then, singsong:

Shitebag if you dinny.

Hades *leaves.*

Òran

Pacing . . . examines the lift more closely, finds the button.

So I just . . . take the lift?

Surely it can't be that easy.
But even if it was that easy
would you even want to see me?

What if you chose to go?
Maybe you already know.
Do you know?

Are you deep in the deep
not held, not kept
but hiding?

Back to pacing.

Or –
could I just be mistaking
your absence for ageing?
Is it natural?
Is my broken heart
just because we've grown apart?

Resolute.

No.
I'll find you in the lowest dark

and somehow break your phone apart.
Maybe we'll separate where ocean starts
and won't both depart on Noah's Ark
but I'll accept it, if you're home from wherever's got you . . .
whoever's got you.

Of course I'll go.
I'd have been a wee brother you see.
I'll come for you and go for me
and go for Mum and drum and whatever's still to come
I'll face it, mud-drunk and journey-wise
and you'll be home.

Òran *enters the lift.*

Lift pings.

Two

Òran
Travelling down
with gloom all gathering round
it suddenly dawns
I haven't pictured where you've gone.

And I find myself thinking:
what will the journey have me do . . .

To the audience:

Are you?

Lift pings.

A floor of glass, black, unblemished.
Slick as buttered baking dish,
slick as windscreens rainiest,
polished up and waiting
for unwitting souls to skate . . . and slip.
The panther black is walls and ceiling
nothing there for watching, seeing,
quiet, clouding,
sighing, prowling.

Peeking over the edge.

Looking over into bottomless depth
I swallow and sweat . . . but step.

Moving around carefully, he traces the edges of a platform.

Until a corner. Right-angle.
Middle-of-the-night angle.
And following still,
the next. And the next . . .
Yes.

I recognise the glassy sheen,
the black, the . . .

EUAN?

Hades
Ok, pal.
This one's a welcome.

Find your footing.
Meet your selves and take them with you. If you can.

You're fuck ugly, Òran.

Chuckles, leaves.

Òran

Pause, looking around, clearly shaken . . . then a fright from below.

A flicker in the floor.
What is this that's sought and found me?
Faces, faces all around me.

Spread low, arms out for balance.

Faces without voices.
I feel naked, toyed with.
But I want to look.
There's something, someone there I recognise.

They're me.

My ugly selves,
uncomfy selves.
Selves best shelved,
selves like skelfs.

A hundred and one expressions:
my glum expressions,
no-fun expressions,
rum expressions,
cum expressions . . .
Fuck-it-I'm-done expressions.

Where are my brave ones?
My early-sun-in-May,
my summer's-day ones,
It'll-all-be-okay ones.

I see how I've looked
in the deep of night, creature-like,
or when I cheered at fights . . .

and I'm back, back, backwards . . .

Shift.

And backing away
I catch the eye of a particular face –
my particular face in a particular place.
A vinegar-burnt, scrunched one.
One that puts me in the kitchen that lunchtime
with Mum in the chair she'd spill spirits on sometimes.
And she's cancelled our trip to get shoes in the sales
and I'm furious, pale, cos Dad's on a food run and I need
new ones.
I want to choose some – *That's what you're meant to let me
do, Mum.*
And she's done her sorrys but she doesn't mean them,
doesn't like me.

Doesn't matter what the day means,
the day Liam would've turned eighteen.
No wonder she only wants to daydream.

Doesn't matter.
Doesn't like me.
And on this day of all days, mid-stamp down the hallway
unplanned as always, I shout:

Me and Dad don't fucking need you, Mum
Neither did Liam, Mum
He needed to leave you, Mum.

Dad says she's injured inside
and since she's injured she hides.

But I had shoes to choose so I cut her.
Over what? Rubbered feet?
So sudden, cheap.
Cut her deep as summer sleep.

I see the face I used to say it,
Twisted as a mountain blackthorn,
Pushing me back, back, backwards.

Mad to see your errors ordered
All your bits of petty torture
All for what?

And the whole spinning world sort of stops.

Shift.

These mes of mine
aren't something I can leave behind.
They're me and maybe always with me
stowaways, walking with me
horrible and not so pretty . . . but me.
And they're coming with me.
Maybe you are fuck ugly, Òran.

At this, the lift lights up once more, signalling progress, he enters.

I smile you into my head

and wonder what's next?

Lift pings.

Three

Òran
I suppose it makes sense –
nighttime, all the way down.
Poison creatures, poison tasks
all the way down.

But I follow you down
and smile you back when I need you,
picture our old lean-to:
my garden, P2.

Hades

Sings 'Rock-a-bye Baby'.

You've got some cheek eh?
Using him for balance.
After what happened.

Tutting.

You sleepy, wee man?
Have a lie-down.
You know you want to.

Shitebag if you dinny.

Leaves.

Òran
I'm no shitebag
I'm not like that.

Feigning confidence.

I'm brave, I'm otherwise engaged,
just one last thing to do before I show myself the cave:
some belly breaths.
Three to be exact, like I like to do in parties

in ensuites or porches,
if I feel out of my depth and don't want seen or noticed.
Three belly breaths and a pinch
on each opposite wrist
like you taught me to as kids.

And smiling you in, I am reminded
night's only night thanks to morning
so I build myself up
to the black we're all born in . . .

Three deep breaths, pinching wrists, eyes shut.

Lift pings.

Opens eyes.

But . . . no.
Honey-glow, lovely, slow lamplight.
Thick carpet . . . rich . . . harmless . . .
and despite it all I discover myself . . .
soothed.

I must be cheap, easily bought even down deep.
How long have I gone without sleep?
The carpet whispers: *weeks.*

So the task is to sleep.
It must be.
I'll do my very best, Euan, trust me.
If all I need to do is doze
you can bet your boots my eyes will close.

Looking around, entering the main chamber.

This *room.*

The many cushions like crocodiles mid-river,
soft and like logs but six thicker.
I'll let the temperature soak me, speak sweetness to
my sore heart,
pull me from the whirlpool and show me where
the shore starts.

Waterfall walnut walls meet the floor
and brace the ceiling and *oh, the ceiling!*
Plum-coloured, purple and blood all-at-once-coloured . . .
And *starred*.

Tracing a 'W' on the ceiling.

Look – Cassiopeia.

I'll sleep.
I'll spend a day, a year at harbour.
Scrub the salt despair I've ladled on in layers
and dream you.
Of course, dream you,
like I always seem to.

Shift, becoming drowsy, curling up perhaps?

Falling from awake
Towards a hardly-knowing sleep
I still soak the lamplight
Forgetting I'm the sheep
And safely on the riverbed
Free of stone or snakes
I start to drift . . .

*A sudden violent vibration, flickering the lights. We should
all get a fright.*

A buzz, an electric shock
Zaps me where I'm lying
Zaps me toe to temple
Like a flying insect frying
Midsummer's still in sky form
I'm hardly faking drowsy
But can't rest with the river
Seeming cold and keen to drown me.

It happens again.

Again it reaches everywhere
A buzz as brief as blinking

Zaps across and through me
Halts my dozing, stops me sinking
When all I want's to drift on
down the river on my cushion
A welcome pit-stop underground
Exhausted, seeking, looking

Delirious.

Autumn . . . Liam . . . Euan?

Pause. Buzzes continue intermittently now, **Òran** *appearing increasingly confused, disturbed.*

Earthquake seven hundred,
Maybe seven thousand
The water's full of crocodiles
I'm prey and I'm surrounded
The carpet's still the softest
I've ever felt below me
But the room has grown oppressive
And it likes me being lonely

Ten minutes here, an hour here
A year, a decade missing
There's no awake or dreaming
In this black hole intermission
I will you still to be here
Wherever it is you are
But start to feel I'll never leave
the riverbed, the stars.

Delirious.

Euan, I'm sorry I could only get this far . . .
I'm desperate.
I'm sorry I've not made it yet.

He slumps again, appearing to resign himself to being stuck here. Then:

Wait . . . wait a sec . . .

Shift. He's realised something.

Whoever's in control here won't ever let me rest,
won't let me carry on unless I'm handicapped at best.
They force you just to lie here, never dozing off,
aching, waiting, sure that who you're looking for is lost.

But I mind a time I heard my parents talking
on the landing.
Years ago, and all this time I couldn't understand it.
Mum was sad and up at night, up as late as three
and through the door I heard Dad
recommend . . . *a cup of tea?*

And now, below the milky way, somewhere underground
I feel the panic ebb away, remembering that sound . . .

*The lift flickers, not fully lighting up yet but hinting he's
on the right track.*

The lift . . .
Not quite . . . but almost!
I'm onto something . . .

To himself:

So buckle up, Òran, there's no reason to linger
and let the clouds blow over, tasting . . . peppermint!
And ginger!
The more you push when something's pushing back you'll
ruin stuff
Instead of holding tighter in the torture, loosen up.

Lift lights up. **Òran** *whoops and cheers and shouts up and around,
as though to* **Hades**.

Bet you thought I'd be stuck here!
Bet you thought I'd give up here!

Oi . . . big man . . . are you out there?
Sad to disappoint you –
I know you want me hurting
so I'm sorry to annoy you –

but it's far too much a hassle
trying to sleep with all your mischief,
so I'll settle for my daydreams
of a cuppa and a biscuit.

To audience, cocky:

I'll catch you lot in a minute.

Saunters into lift.

Lift pings.

Four

Hades

A sudden, wordless growl/scream: he's furious at **Òran**'s
progression.

Clever clogs, eh?
He thinks he's clever?

I'll show him fucking clever.

He'll need to show himself.

Show himself and share his shame.

To an audience member:

What will he need to do?

'Share his shame.'

Too fucking right he will.

Lift pings.

Òran
It's quiet out here.
Quiet as books.
Quiet as standing stones.
Quiet as bones,
but not silent . . . not quite . . .

Such everything-nothing's heavy and pulsing,
echoing, beckoning.
The silence rustles, runs off the low ceiling
and down the walls to pile like Canadian snow.
I heard they get loads.

Moving deeper still,
the dark gathers behind me,
inside me, shoves my shoulders

like a school bully.

But even sleepless, lead-legged,
I smile you into my head,
remembering when we got up in my dad's attic,
hoods up on our black jackets.
We made spiders with our fingers
and gasped as they grew bigger.
We dug the *dark* for adventure.
So here, again, although I might look cornered,
I push forward . . .

Up close to people.

and again . . . faces,
but not mine this time.

Thirsty-eyed, broad faces,
thin, sharp, soft faces.
Silent, zip-mouthed,
all different, all listening,
long fingered, listening.

They want something of me.
They want me tested, questioned,
spun, shrunk and sent downward different.
And I want you home,
I want you home I'm so insistent –

So here I am!

Up in individual faces, frantic.

What d'you *need?*
What d'you *eat?*
What d'you *keep?*

Arriving at the selected audience member:

What do I need to do?

Audience member: 'Share your shame.'

Pause, significant shift, confession.

Òran
Have it then, I'll offer it
There's one I've had since twelve
A memory, a something
I can barely tell myself
I'm careful, I've been careful with it
Chiefly out of shame
Neatly, it's been hidden
But it's in me all the same

Take it . . . here,
Have it then, I'll offer it
I'd rather not, I'd rather stop
I'm sure that much is obvious
It's lived in deeper corners
than I've visited for ages
I never wanted all those
older boys to see me naked

Early on in big school
An innocent mistake
To lend a friend my phone
To send an album during break
Part of things and proud of it
Keen to share my music
Forgot about the camera
Forgot just how I'd used it . . .

Showed myself myself
And showed the full-length mirror too
Showed the room, showed the walls,
Clothes and pairs of shoes,
Touched myself and watched it
with a shiver and a twist
Showed it to my camera
Wasn't thinking of the risk.

Pulled along by school days
Learning to survive
Learning how to get on

with the older boys and thrive
Left a friend my phone
and said I'd meet him after lunch
Found him in a circle
Showing everyone my stunt.

Showing them me trying on the world
Thin and bald-bitted
Showing them me thrusting out my hips
In the tall mirror
Showing them me private
and my privates with delight
Saw me see them watching
And got whispery with the night like . . .

Òran made a porno
Òran made a porno
Òran made a porno

Hades

Arrives to lead/cajole the audience to chant:

Òran made a porno
Òran made a porno
Òran made a porno

Òran, *bent, shaken, finds himself in the lift as the chant collapses into* **Hades**' *laughter.*

Lift pings.

We see **Òran** *in the lift, lit, shaking, vulnerable as it carries him down.*

Five

Òran

Steps out into a cacophony of layered message alerts, pings, bells, vibrations, etc., constant.

Here we are.
No place for the living. A place for the not-living.

Hades
Hiya, Òran.
Welcome, wee man.
Mi casa es su casa.

Òran
So many people. Sat in line.
The longest line.
They're not looking at me –
I try to breathe and do it badly, gaspy.

They're people but not people.
People but wrong people,
long-gone-people,
bent-necked, swan people,
drowned, never-found pond-people.

And even shoulder to shoulder,
they don't notice each other.
Cheek-to-blue-lit-cheek, none are still,
all are ill up nightmare hill.
Always looking –
only looking –
down.

This Deep Downstairs is rock and oil, fog and soil
but somehow . . . phones.
The homes from homes.
They sing their sounds

and tweak and tease
and all the broken thumbs still flick and push
and grip and itch
and move and use
and use.
and use.

And of course: cables.
Chargers.
Dead tails buzzing, plugging,
all down the line and into the dark,
crawling out from under the trembling guests
like tapeworms and burrowed into stone floor.

Feeding tubes.
Umbilicals.
Digital.

Pause.

The line mimes a centipede:
back-to-back, folded souls the torso,
curling cables the twitching limbs.
A snaking, aching, wriggling thing.

Shouting, to the room:

All these rooms I've been through
. . . has anyone seen you?

EUAN?

Frantic, pointing, targeting particular audience members.

You! Soft of jaw and thick of hair
I'm with you in your disrepair and grab your wrists
to wake you up, to shake you
but the more I pull the more you sit.

You! High of cheekbones, young in years
I'm sad to see you stuck in here and prod your chest
to wake you up, to shake you
but the more I push the more you rest.

You! Thin of eyebrows, long of arms
I find you in this awful farm and slap your face
to wake you up, to shake you
but the more I hit the more you wait.

Fruitless, collapses panting.

Limp, I sit and think
of the furthest we ever walked together:
your house to the golf course in awful weather,
hoods up, yellow scarves
up and round the reservoir . . . and back.

Back up on his feet!

If this line is that long I'll do it.
Even twice that long I'll do it.
But what's too long?
Where do I stop?
Do I walk so far I wear my feet off?
Imagine not having feet to lead you home with.
Hopeless.

Will I ever find you?
Maybe I'll never find you.

I've come for you
and come for me,
and for another hundred reasons,
somehow maybe come for wolves
and come for Liam.

It's just not the same with **Òran**.

Pause, lull, low.

And then . . .
Fuck.
I'm hearing it.

It's been yours since high school
I know because *I've* been yours since high school.

When you chose it, when you set it, I knew I'd never forget it.
Your alert, when messaged:
AHAAA!

Òran's *suddenly frantic, spinning, trying to spot Euan,*
then **Hades** *interrupts.*

Hades
That's a boy, Òran.
Have to hand it to you, wee man.
Thought you were all pastry no pie.
You found him.
Wee Euan.

Òran
And what's it to you?
What are you gonna do?

Hades
I've a mind to turn you stone, ya wee dick.

Pause, chuckles.

But you've lost a lot, haven't you, pal.
Just the way I want it.

Òran
I know you're in charge here,
living it large here.

So what now?
What next?
Can I wake him?
Take him?

Hades
I'm gonny miss you, Òran.

Take him?
By all means.
I dare ye.
Win his focus.

One look at the phone and he's bones.
If you lose he's lunch, wee man, he's toast.

Oh . . . here . . . Òran?

Tell him.

Shitebag if you dinny . . .

Laughs, leaves.

Six

Òran

Savour this moment.

It's you.
Squeezed between two others
like a book there's no room for.

Euan –
thinner, bruised . . .
but *you.*

And here beneath high ceilings,
on stone floors, death-deep –
You don't see me.

It seems the toughest task
is to make you see me.

Òran *animated, more aggressive, trying to rouse him.*

COME HOME? PLEASE!
WHAT ABOUT AUTUMN LEAVES?
C'MON! IT'S ME!

I slap and tug, implore and twist.
Pull and snatch, roar and spit.
Cut your skin in clawing rescue –
you took so fucking *long* to get to . . .

Slumped, mumbled, rambling.

Mum.
Forgive her.
Miss her.
Hip flasks.
Miss Dad.

Pause.

I'm no shitebag,
I'm not like that.

So I've to tell you.
Here, ignored on deepest shores.
I need you back from deepest black.

I'd have been a wee brother you see.
And no matter what colour the leaves
you were sort of like that brother to me.

When my dog died
I felt it cut half as deep
cos I stayed with you half the week.

I have to tell you.

When your phone bruised you
And I started to lose you
I felt everything shift.

And when everything shifted
I did what you didn't.
I went and stuck close to the boys
who seemed biggest.

Pause.

When you started snapping at my hi's and why's
and blinking quicker, skipping dinner
to cross between worlds,
I found new places to spend autumn.
I folded smaller, backed into strange places
with new friends who had vague faces
new friends who didn't like me
new friends who didn't like you.
I found myself in virtual rooms
where error soon meant lead balloon
and a lifetime in the stocks,
And I started using words
like *fat* and *cock*.

I *have* to tell you.
And I missed you,
but I needed somewhere safe since
by then you weren't saying things
and my new friends were saying things
things that felt the safest things –
whispering till I hated you,
whispers, and I saved a few
and I missed you
but still found your phone
on my phone
and wrote . . .

I wrote –

I wrote
You should drink bleach
to try and sleep
and film it for science week,
and I'd get the whole street
to donate a fiver each.
When you refused, confused
I wrote
'Fine, no problem
Here's the other option
We'll leak pictures of you wanking
Tryina practise with a condom.'
I knew you'd sent them.
I hadn't forgotten.

Pause.

And when you told me this ugly thing,
told me my ugly thing,
your face did a crumple thing.
Your face did a hundred things
none of them comforting.

I feel it now for certain,
that the phones alone don't sentence,

that they're only a reflection
of a version of a person.

Òran *spent, laid bare.*

Euan sees **Òran.**

Òran

Stunned, incredulous.

You see me.
You're looking.
Eyes I've known since primary school
It's finally you.

But Alan Partridge shouts again
and all at once I know I've lost you,
brace myself, I know I've got to,
know you're set to leave again,
entitled not to be my friend
but . . . *no.*

A shiver comes and goes
and though your thumbs still tense and flick
your eyes stay on me, fixed.
Your shoulders rise and toes curl over,
body bound by learned behaviour
but breaking from the same old script
your eyes stay on me, fixed.

To himself:

Keep him looking.
Quick, Òran, quick.

Euan.
Come home.
It's new there without you.
The walks to work, the smoke breaks,
autumn's still nice and fresh
but I like it less without you.

Euan.
Mind the hospital?
Blue hands cos we didn't wear gloves?
You got kissed at the skate park!

And suddenly your hand's in mine.
You're looking at me.
I stand and dig my heels in,
brace and pull and break the rules
and drag you from the longest line of trodden minds
and high above the others like the tallest pine
you stand.
Sway.
Stand.
You're looking at me.
Keep looking.

Euan.
The lean-to.
My garden, P2.
Mind?
Show me with your eyes.
You do? Me too!

They move off, through the cave, towards the lift.

If you don't watch your phone
I've got you home.

We travel the grey cave together at an ancient pace.
Bicep to bicep in this ancient place.
Stay awake.

The centipede scars the dark beside us
and I notice as we pass each guest
eyes meet us, flash, for just a sec.
Eyes that never leave the screens
sense you breaking deep routine.

The leaves are changing,
and I can taste the hot tea of home.

Lift lights up, signalling he's passed the test.

Lift pings.

They're in the lift together, travelling up.

Keep looking at me.

There I am, Euan:
Òran made a porno, Òran made a porno.

There I am, Euan:
sweating, half-sleeping but not sleeping
half dreaming but not dreaming

There I am: fuck ugly.

But seeing all I've done's done something to me.
It's not quite like I'm suddenly free . . .
but freer.

And facing it, taking it . . . d'you know something?
I'm not hating it.

Let this sink in.

You're looking at me
and I brace,
and push,
and stand,
and reach up for the world,
Our world.

And Euan –
you look at me and shudder,
half-smile,
and shrug.

And into my mind I gather
All the autumn leaves above.

Lift pings.

Lift opens onto the world again, then:

Euan?

A phone rings suddenly, cutting through the space.

Hades

Laughing – then cut to black.

Discover. Read. Listen. Watch.

A NEW WAY TO ENGAGE WITH PLAYS

This award-winning digital library features over 3,000 playtexts, 400 audio plays, 300 hours of video and 360 scholarly books.

Playtexts published by Methuen Drama, The Arden Shakespeare, Faber & Faber, Playwrights Canada Press, Aurora Metro Books and Nick Hern Books.

Audio Plays from L.A. Theatre Works featuring classic and modern works from the oeuvres of leading American playwrights.

Video collections including films of live performances from the RSC, The Globe and The National Theatre, as well as acting masterclasses and BBC feature films and documentaries.

FIND OUT MORE:

www.dramaonlinelibrary.com • @dramaonlinelib

Methuen Drama Modern Plays

include

Bola Agbaje
Edward Albee
Ayad Akhtar
Jean Anouilh
John Arden
Peter Barnes
Sebastian Barry
Clare Barron
Alistair Beaton
Brendan Behan
Edward Bond
William Boyd
Bertolt Brecht
Howard Brenton
Amelia Bullmore
Anthony Burgess
Leo Butler
Jim Cartwright
Lolita Chakrabarti
Caryl Churchill
Lucinda Coxon
Tim Crouch
Shelagh Delaney
Ishy Din
Claire Dowie
David Edgar
David Eldridge
Dario Fo
Michael Frayn
John Godber
James Graham
David Greig
John Guare
Lauren Gunderson
Peter Handke
David Harrower
Jonathan Harvey
Robert Holman
David Ireland
Sarah Kane

Barrie Keeffe
Jasmine Lee-Jones
Anders Lustgarten
Duncan Macmillan
David Mamet
Patrick Marber
Martin McDonagh
Arthur Miller
Alistair McDowall
Tom Murphy
Phyllis Nagy
Anthony Neilson
Peter Nichols
Ben Okri
Joe Orton
Vinay Patel
Joe Penhall
Luigi Pirandello
Stephen Poliakoff
Lucy Prebble
Peter Quilter
Mark Ravenhill
Philip Ridley
Willy Russell
Jackie Sibblies Drury
Sam Shepard
Martin Sherman
Chris Shinn
Wole Soyinka
Simon Stephens
Kae Tempest
Anne Washburn
Laura Wade
Theatre Workshop
Timberlake Wertenbaker
Roy Williams
Snoo Wilson
Frances Ya-Chu Cowhig
Benjamin Zephaniah

Methuen Drama Contemporary Dramatists

include

John Arden (two volumes)
Arden & D'Arcy
Peter Barnes (three volumes)
Sebastian Barry
Mike Bartlett
Clare Barron
Brad Birch
Dermot Bolger
Edward Bond (ten volumes)
Howard Brenton (two volumes)
Leo Butler (two volumes)
Richard Cameron
Jim Cartwright
Caryl Churchill (two volumes)
Complicite
Sarah Daniels (two volumes)
Nick Darke
David Edgar (three volumes)
David Eldridge (two volumes)
Ben Elton
Per Olov Enquist
Dario Fo (two volumes)
Michael Frayn (four volumes)
John Godber (four volumes)
Paul Godfrey
James Graham (two volumes)
David Greig
John Guare
Lee Hall (two volumes)
Katori Hall
Peter Handke
Jonathan Harvey (two volumes)
Iain Heggie
Israel Horovitz
Declan Hughes
Terry Johnson (three volumes)
Sarah Kane
Barrie Keeffe
Bernard-Marie Koltès (two
volumes)
Franz Xaver Kroetz
Kwame Kwei-Armah
David Lan
Bryony Lavery
Deborah Levy
Doug Lucie

Alistair MacDowall
Sabrina Mahfouz
David Mamet (six volumes)
Patrick Marber
Martin McDonagh
Duncan McLean
David Mercer (two volumes)
Anthony Minghella (two volumes)
Rory Mullarkey
Tom Murphy (six volumes)
Phyllis Nagy
Anthony Neilson (three volumes)
Peter Nichol (two volumes)
Philip Osment
Gary Owen
Louise Page
Stewart Parker (two volumes)
Joe Penhall (two volumes)
Stephen Poliakoff (three volumes)
David Rabe (two volumes)
Mark Ravenhill (three volumes)
Christina Reid
Philip Ridley (two volumes)
Willy Russell
Eric-Emmanuel Schmitt
Ntozake Shange
Sam Shepard (two volumes)
Martin Sherman (two volumes)
Christopher Shinn (two volumes)
Joshua Sobel
Wole Soyinka (two volumes)
Simon Stephens (five volumes)
Shelagh Stephenson
David Storey (three volumes)
C. P. Taylor
Sue Townsend
Judy Upton (two volumes)
Michel Vinaver (two volumes)
Arnold Wesker (two volumes)
·Peter Whelan
Michael Wilcox
Roy Williams (four volumes)
David Williamson
Snoo Wilson (two volumes)
David Wood (two volumes)
Victoria Wood

Methuen Drama Student Editions

Alan Ayckbourn *Confusions* • **Mike Bartlett** *Earthquakes in London* • **Aphra Behn** *The Rover* • **Alice Birch** *Revolt. She Said. Revolt Again* • **Edward Bond** *Lear* • *Saved* • **Bertolt Brecht** *The Caucasian Chalk Circle* • *Fear and Misery in the Third Reich* • *The Good Person of Szechwan* • *Life of Galileo* • *Mother Courage and her Children* • *The Resistible Rise of Arturo Ui* • *The Threepenny Opera* • **Jon Brittain** *Rotterdam* • **Georg Büchner** *Woyzeck* • **Anton Chekhov** *The Cherry Orchard* • *The Seagull* • *Three Sisters* • *Uncle Vanya* • **Caryl Churchill** *Serious Money* • *Top Girls* • **Shelagh Delaney** *A Taste of Honey* • **Inua Ellams** *Barber Shop Chronicles* • **Euripides** *Elektra* • *Medea* • **Dario Fo** *Accidental Death of an Anarchist* • **Michael Frayn** *Copenhagen* • **John Galsworthy** *Strife* • **Nikolai Gogol** *The Government Inspector* • **Carlo Goldoni** *A Servant to Two Masters* • **James Graham** *This House* • **Tanika Gupta** *The Empress* • **Katori Hall** *The Mountaintop* • **Lorraine Hansberry** *A Raisin in the Sun* • **Robert Holman** *Across Oka* • **Henrik Ibsen** *A Doll's House* • *Ghosts* • *Hedda Gabler* • **Sarah Kane** *4.48 Psychosis* • *Blasted* • **Charlotte Keatley** *My Mother Said I Never Should* • **Dennis Kelly** *DNA* • **Bernard Kops** *Dreams of Anne Frank* • **Federico García Lorca** *Blood Wedding* • *Doña Rosita the Spinster* (bilingual edition) • *The House of Bernarda Alba* (bilingual edition) • *Yerma* (bilingual edition) • **David Mamet** *Glengarry Glen Ross* • *Oleanna* • **Patrick Marber** *Closer* • **John Marston** *The Malcontent* • **Martin McDonagh** *The Lieutenant of Inishmore* • *The Lonesome West* • *The Beauty Queen of Leenane* • *The Cripple of Inishmaan* • **Alistair McDowall** *Pomona* • **John McGrath** *The Cheviot, the Stag and the Black, Black Oil* • **Arthur Miller** *All My Sons* • *The Crucible* • *A View from the Bridge* • *Death of a Salesman* • *The Price* • *After the Fall* • *The Last Yankee* • *A Memory of Two Mondays* • *Broken Glass* • *Incident at Vichy* • *The American Clock* • *The Ride Down Mt. Morgan* • **Joe Orton** *Loot* • **Joe Penhall** *Blue/Orange* • **Luigi Pirandello** *Six Characters in Search of an Author* • **Lucy Prebble** *Enron* • **Mark Ravenhill** *Shopping and F***ing* • **Reginald Rose** *Twelve Angry Men* • **Willy Russell** *Blood Brothers* • *Educating Rita* • **Lemn Sissay** Benjamin Zephaniah's *Refugee Boy* • **Sophocles** *Antigone* • *Oedipus the King* • **Wole Soyinka** *Death and the King's Horseman* • **Simon Stephens** *Punk Rock* • *Pornography* • **Shelagh Stephenson** *The Memory of Water* • **August Strindberg** *Miss Julie* • **J. M. Synge** *The Playboy of the Western World* • **Kae Tempest** *Wasted* • **Theatre Workshop** *Oh What a Lovely War* • **Laura Wade** *Posh* • **Frank Wedekind** *Spring Awakening* • **Timberlake Wertenbaker** *Our Country's Good* • **Arnold Wesker** *The Merchant* • **Peter Whelan** *The Accrington Pals* • **Oscar Wilde** *The Importance of Being Earnest* • **Roy Williams** *Sing Yer Heart Out for the Lads* • **Tennessee Williams** *A Streetcar Named Desire* • *The Glass Menagerie* • *Cat on a Hot Tin Roof* • *Sweet Bird of Youth*

Methuen Drama
Classical Greek Dramatists

Aeschylus Plays: One
(Persians, Seven Against Thebes, Suppliants,
Prometheus Bound)

Aeschylus Plays: Two
(Oresteia: Agamemnon, Libation-Bearers, Eumenides)

Aristophanes Plays: One
(Acharnians, Knights, Peace, Lysistrata)

Aristophanes Plays: Two
(Wasps, Clouds, Birds, Festival Time, Frogs)

Aristophanes & Menander: New Comedy
(Women in Power, Wealth, The Malcontent,
The Woman from Samos)

Euripides Plays: One
(Medea, The Phoenician Women, Bacchae)

Euripides Plays: Two
(Hecuba, The Women of Troy, Iphigeneia at Aulis, Cyclops)

Euripides Plays: Three
(Alkestis, Helen, Ion)

Euripides Plays: Four
(Elektra, Orestes, Iphigeneia in Tauris)

Euripides Plays: Five
(Andromache, Herakles' Children, Herakles)

Euripides Plays: Six
(Hippolytos, Suppliants, Rhesos)

Sophocles Plays: One
(Oedipus the King, Oedipus at Colonus, Antigone)

Sophocles Plays: Two
(Ajax, Women of Trachis, Electra, Philoctetes)

For a complete listing of
Methuen Drama titles, visit:
www.bloomsbury.com/drama

Follow us on Twitter and keep up to date
with our news and publications
@MethuenDrama